Ve

50 Healthy & Delicious Recipes For A Ketogenic Vegan Diet

By Karen McAdams

Table of Contents

Introduction

Veganism is an ideology based on the premise that all living creatures, including animals, should be respected, and that the killing and consumption of animals and animal-based ingredients breaches this premise.

On the other hand, a ketogenic is a way of eating that was initially developed to minimize epileptic attacks. Later, it was discovered that it also helps with weight loss.

A ketogenic diet promotes the consumption of mainly fats, and some protein, while maintaining very low levels of carbohydrates.

With a bit of planning, a vegan or ketogenic diet may not be difficult to follow by themselves. However, a vegan AND ketogenic diet... is that actually possible?

Yes!

While you'll undoubtedly be more limited in your food choices than most other people, a ketogenic vegan diet can still contain plenty of tasty and nutritious meals, and the proof is in this recipe book.

All of the included recipes are neatly numbered and organized into 5 different categories: Breakfast, Lunch, Dinner, Snacks and Desserts.

We hope you enjoy exploring the healthy, fatty goodness of the vegan keto world.

Happy cooking, and bon appétit!

Breakfast Recipes

1. Fruity Chia Pudding

Fruity Chia pudding is the perfect breakfast when you need something fruity, healthy, and fast. Don't be put off by the word 'fruity', though, as the carbs are still kept low.

Preparation time: 20 minutes

Serves: 1

Ingredients:
- ¾ cup unsweetened almond milk
- ¼ cup filtered water
- 2 tablespoons whole white Chia seeds
- 1 tablespoon almond butter
- ¼ cup fresh raspberries

Directions:
1. Mix almond milk, water, chia seeds, and almond butter in a bowl. If you prefer a smoother texture, blend the ingredients in a food blender.
2. Place the chia blend aside for 15 minutes.
3. In the meantime, blend raspberries in a food blender until smooth.
4. Strain the raspberry puree through a fine sieve and discard the seeds.
5. Spread the raspberry puree over the chia seed blend and serve.

6. For a more enjoyable experience, you can chill it before serving.

Nutrition analysis:
- High in iron
- High in calcium

2. Green Avocado Pancakes

These wonderful pancakes are made with ripe avocado, spinach, and almond flour. These green beauties are some of the healthiest pancakes you'll ever try.

Preparation time: 10 minutes

Cooking time: 10 minutes

Serves: 4

Ingredients:

- 1 avocado
- 1 cup packed fresh baby spinach
- ½ cup almond flour
- ¼ teaspoon aluminum-free baking powder
- 1 flax egg*
- ¼ cup unsweetened almond milk
- 1 pinch Himalayan salt
- Coconut oil, to fry
-

*Flax egg: combine 2 tablespoons ground flax seeds with ¼ cup filtered water.

Place aside for 10 minutes or until thickened.

Directions:

1. Cut the avocado in half and remove the stone, then peel the avocado and cut into thin slices.
2. Place the avocado slices, spinach, flax egg, and almond milk

in a food blender.

3. Blend until smooth. Transfer the batter into a medium bowl.
4. Fold in almond flour, baking powder, and salt.
5. Brush a non-stick skillet with melted coconut oil.
6. Pour 2-3 tablespoons of the batter into heated skillet.
7. Cook the pancakes on medium heat for 2 minutes. Flip gently (because the pancakes are very soft) and cook further for 2 minutes. Repeat with the remaining batter.
8. Serve warm with desired topping, or vegetables.

Nutrition analysis:

- High in vitamin A
- Moderate in potassium.
- Moderate in dietary fiber

3. Savory Crepes With Mushroom & Asparagus Filling

Rich mushroom-asparagus filling, wrapped in thin, low-carb crepes and with decadent cashew-lemon sauce. A yummy start to the day!

Preparation time: 30 minutes

Cooking time: 20 minutes

Serves: 4

Ingredients:

For the crepes:
- 3 flax eggs*
- 1 ¼ cup blanched almond flour
- 1 tablespoon sifted coconut flour
- 1 teaspoon aluminum-free baking powder
- 1 cup unsweetened almond milk
- 2 tablespoons olive oil
- 1 pinch Himalayan salt

For the filling:
- 12 asparagus spears, trimmed
- 2 cups sliced mushrooms
- 3 tablespoons olive oil
- 1 sprig thyme, leaves removed

- 1 good pinch Himalayan salt

For the sauce;

- ¾ cup cashew butter
- 2 tablespoons lime juice
- 2 tablespoons lemon juice
- Salt, to taste
- White pepper, to taste

*Flax egg: combine 2 tablespoons ground flax seeds with ¼ cup filtered water. Place aside for 10 minutes or until thickened – equals one egg

Directions:

1. Make the sauce; place all ingredients in a food processor. Process the ingredients until smooth. Chill in a fridge before use.
2. Make the crepes; combine all the crepes ingredients in a bowl, except the olive oil. If needed add some more liquid.
3. Place the batter in a fridge for 30 minutes.
4. Heat some of the olive oil in a large pan.
5. Pour ¼ cup of the batter into the skillet and swirl the pan to distribute the batter evenly.
6. Cook until bubbles appear on the surface. Flip carefully and cook for 1 minute.
7. Repeat with remaining batter and keep the pancakes warm.
8. Make the filling; Heat olive oil in a pan over medium-high heat.
9. Add the sliced mushrooms and thyme and cook for 5 minutes.
10. Add the asparagus and cook until crisp-tender, for 2-3 minutes. Season with salt.
11. To assemble; place a pancake on a plate. Fill with some prepared filling and fold the pancake sides over the filling.
12. Drizzle with sauce and serve.

Nutrition analysis:
- High in omega 3
- High in calcium
- Moderate in protein

4. Limey Waffles With Coconut Cream

A refreshing, easy-to-make and satisfying breakfast experience.

Preparation time: 15 minutes

Cooking time: 10 minutes

Serves: 4

Ingredients:

For the waffles:
- 2 flax eggs*
- 2 tablespoons almond butter
- 1 ½ cups almond flour
- 2 tablespoons sifted coconut flour
- ¼ cup unsweetened almond milk
- 2 tablespoons lime juice
- Coconut oil, to brush the iron
- Desired sweetener, a combination of Erythritol and stevia, to taste

For the coconut cream:
- 15oz. can coconut milk (chilled in a fridge overnight)
- 1 teaspoon lime zest

*Flax egg: combine 2 tablespoons ground flax seeds with ¼ cup filtered water. Place aside for 10 minutes or until thickened – equals one egg

Directions:

1. Make the coconut cream; chill the coconut milk in a fridge overnight. Remove carefully from the fridge without shaking.
2. Open the can and remove the coconut cream solids. Place the coconut cream solids in a chilled bowl.
3. Beat coconut cream with lime zest, and desired sweetener using an electric mixer until fluffy. Store in a fridge until ready to use.
4. Make the waffles; combine all ingredients in a bowl.
5. Heat the waffle iron. Brush the iron gently with coconut oil.
6. Pour some of the prepared batter onto the iron and cook for 3-4 minutes.
7. Serve the waffles with a dollop of coconut cream.

Nutrition analysis:

- High in manganese
- Moderate in saturated fat
- Low in sodium

5. Eggplant Guac Stack

This nutritious and satiating meal is made with eggplant and homemade guacamole. If you do it right, you'll end up with some crunchy and creamy goodness.

Preparation time: 40 minutes

Cooking time: 10 minutes

Serves: 4

Ingredients:

- 1 lb. eggplant, trimmed and sliced into ½-inch thick rounds
- ½ cup ground almonds
- ¼ cup ground macadamia nuts
- 1 teaspoon dried basil
- ½ cup flax seeds
- 1 cup filtered water
- ½ teaspoon Himalayan salt
- ½ teaspoon freshly ground white pepper
- ¼ cup melted coconut oil

For the guacamole:

- 2 small avocados
- 3 tablespoons lime juice
- 2 tablespoons freshly chopped chives
- Sea salt and pepper, to taste

Directions:

1. Make the guacamole; cut avocados in half and remove the stone.
2. Peel and slice the avocados and place into a small bowl.
3. Drizzle with lemon juice and season to taste with salt and pepper.
4. Mash the avocado with a fork and sprinkle with chives. Cover and store in a refrigerator until ready to use.
5. Make the eggplants; sprinkle eggplant slices with salt and place in a colander for 20 minutes.
6. Squeeze to remove excess liquid.
7. In a bowl, combine flax seeds and water.
8. Place aside for 15 minutes until thickened and gelatinous.
9. Combine almond flour with white pepper in a shallow dish, and place macadamia nuts in a separate shallow dish.
10. Heat coconut oil in a pan over medium-high heat.
11. Dredge eggplant slices in almond flour, dip into flax mixture and coat with macadamia nuts.
12. Place the eggplant slices into heated oil and fry for 2 minutes per side. Place onto a plate.
13. To assemble; spread some guacamole over one eggplant slice and sandwich with the second eggplant slice. Repeat with remaining slices and guacamole.
14. Serve warm.

Nutrition analysis:

- High in dietary fiber
- High in iron
- High in vitamin C
- High in vitamin E
- Moderate in vitamin K

6. Mushrooms In Spinach-Coconut Cream

Mushrooms and spinach pair perfectly, and this dish is proof of it. With the addition of tofu, it's a bit higher in protein than most other meals.

Preparation time: 10 minutes

Cooking time: 15 minutes

Serves: 4

Ingredients:

- ½ (15oz.) package silken tofu
- 1 ½ lb. sliced brown mushrooms
- 3 tablespoons coconut oil
- Sea salt, to taste

For the spinach:

- ½ lb. baby spinach
- 2 minced garlic cloves
- ½ cup unsweetened coconut cream
- 2 tablespoons coconut oil
- 1 pinch nutmeg
- Sea salt and black pepper, to taste

Directions:

1. Prepare the mushrooms; heat coconut oil in a medium pan over medium-high heat.

2. Add mushrooms and season to taste.
3. Cook the mushrooms for 6-7 minutes, stirring until soft.
4. In the meantime, mash the silken tofu with a fork.
5. Top the mushrooms with silken tofu and cook for 3-4 minutes.
6. Place aside and keep warm.
7. Make the spinach; heat coconut oil in a medium pan over medium-high heat.
8. Add garlic and cook until fragrant, for 30-40 seconds.
9. Toss in spinach and cook until wilted.
10. Add the coconut cream, nutmeg, and season to taste.
11. Stir well and remove from heat. Place the mushrooms and tofu in a bowl. Top with spinach.
12. Serve warm.

Nutrition analysis:
-   High in protein
-   High in dietary fiber
-   High in vitamin A

7. Rich Carob Protein Smoothie

Smoothie is a perfect "fast food" you can prepare within only a few minutes.

With a careful combination of ingredients, smoothies will fill you up for a long time, just like any other breakfast.

Preparation time: 5 minutes

Serves: 1 big smoothie

Ingredients:

- ¼ cup almond or coconut milk
- ¼ cup water
- 2 tablespoon cocoa butter
- 2 tablespoons unsweetened coconut cream
- 1 tablespoon carob powder
- 1 scoop mixed plant protein powder or soy protein powder
- 1 tablespoon macadamia oil or MCT oil
- ½ cup ice
- 4 drops Stevia
- ½ teaspoon Ceylon cinnamon

Directions:
1. Place all ingredients in a food blender.
2. Blend until smooth.
3. Serve immediately.

Nutrition analysis:

- High in protein
- High in vitamin K

8. Coconut Cauliflower Porridge

Sometimes, you just need some comfort food for breakfast, and what is more comforting than warm porridge? We bring you a ketogenic and vegan-approved porridge!

Preparation time: 10 minutes + inactive time

Cooking time: 10 minutes

Serves: 4

Ingredients:
- ½ head cauliflower, just florets, discard stems
- ¼ cup chia seeds
- ¾ cup coconut flakes
- 3 tablespoons coconut oil
- 1 ½ cup coconut milk
- ½ teaspoon Ceylon cinnamon
- Sweetener, like stevia to taste

Directions:
1. Preheat oven to 425F and line a baking sheet with baking paper.
2. Place cauliflower florets in a food processor with 1 tablespoon coconut oil.
3. Process until the cauliflower is rice-like in consistency.
4. Spread the cauliflower onto lined baking sheet and roast for 8-10 minutes.
5. In the meantime, combine chia seeds, coconut flakes, 1 cup coconut milk, and cinnamon in a bowl.
6. Add the cauliflower and give it a good stir. Cover and refrigerate for at least two hours.

7. Just before serving, combine remaining coconut oil, remaining coconut milk, and desired amount of Stevia in a food blender.
8. Blend until emulsified.
9. Pour the emulsified coconut oil over the cauliflower and stir gently. Serve immediately.

Nutrition analysis:
- High in manganese
- Moderate in copper
- Moderate in iron

9. Bread With Herbed Butter

A lot of people who go on ketogenic diets really miss the consistency of freshly-baked bread. If you're one of them, this recipe will help alleviate some of your cravings. Give this a try with some fresh avocado to serve, and you won't be disappointed!

Preparation time: 20 minutes

Cooking time: 60 minutes

Serves: 10 slices

Ingredients:

For the buns:

-   ½ cup drained firm tofu
-   3 tablespoons ground flax seeds
-   ¾ cup coconut milk
-   ½ cup psyllium husk
-   1 teaspoon aluminum-free baking powder
-   1 good pinch Himalayan salt

For the butter:

-   4 tablespoons blanched almond flour
-   1 teaspoon nutritional yeast
-   ¼ cup unsweetened almond milk or soy milk
-   ½ cup melted and cooled coconut oil

- 2 tablespoons extra-virgin olive oil
- ½ teaspoon cider vinegar
- ½ teaspoon Himalayan salt
- 1 teaspoon fresh chopped thyme
- 1 teaspoon fresh chopped basil

To serve:

- 1 pitted, peeled, and sliced avocado

Directions:

1. Make the butter; blend almonds, nutritional yeast, almond milk, vinegar, herbs, and salt in a food blender until smooth.
2. While the blender is running on low, add coconut oil, followed by extra-virgin olive oil.
3. Continue blending until you have a velvety mixture. Transfer into a freezer-friendly glass jar and apply the lid.
4. Freeze until you make buns.
5. Make the buns; Preheat oven to 350F and line a baking sheet with a parchment paper.
6. Place the drained tofu in a food blender. Blend until smooth.
7. Add the remaining ingredients and blend until combined.
8. Drop the batter into mounds on a baking sheet. Bake for 55-60 minutes or until browned.
9. Serve warm with herbed butter and slices of avocado.

Nutrition analysis:

- High in thiamin
- Moderate in omega 3
- Moderate in vitamin E

10. Almond Butter & Red Currant Muffins

Sweet, fluffy, and made with delicious red currants. A gourmet-like breakfast experience.

Preparation time: 15 minutes

Cooking time: 22 minutes

Serves: 12 muffins

Ingredients:

- ¾ cup coconut flour
- ¾ cup almond flour
- ½ cup almond butter
- 1 teaspoon aluminum-free baking soda
- ½ cup fresh red currants
- ½ cup almond milk
- 2 tablespoons coconut oil
- 2 flax eggs*
- Stevia + Erythritol, to taste
- 1 teaspoon pure vanilla extract

*Flax egg: combine 2 tablespoons ground flax seeds with ¼ cup filtered water. Place aside for 10 minutes or until thickened.

Directions:

1. Preheat oven to 350F and line 12-hole muffin tin with paper liners.
2. In a medium bowl, whisk together coconut flour, almond

flour, and baking soda.
3. Make the flax eggs and place aside.
4. In a separate bowl, whisk together almond butter, almond milk, coconut oil, Stevia, Erythritol, vanilla, and flax eggs.
5. Fold the dry ingredients into the wet ingredients and stir to combine. If you feel the batter is too dry, add some almond milk.
6. Gently fold in red currants and divide batter between muffin liners.
7. Bake the muffins for 20-22 minutes.
8. Serve at room temperature.

Nutrition analysis:
- High in vitamin E
- High in protein
- Moderate in omega 3

Lunch Recipes

11. Palm Heart Tacos

This is the perfect recipe for vegans on a ketogenic diet. Besides being low-carb, it is perfectly seasoned with well-balanced flavors.

Preparation time: 20 minutes

Cooking time: 5 minutes

Serves: 4

Ingredients:

For the filling:

-   2 14oz. cans palm hearts, rinsed and drained
-   4 tablespoons coconut aminos
-   1 teaspoon chili sauce
-   2 tablespoons olive oil
-   1 teaspoon minced garlic

For the sauce:

-   2 cups hemp seeds
-   ½ cup filtered water
-   ½ cup fresh lemon juice
-   1 pinch Himalayan salt

For the tacos:

- 1 head lettuce
- ½ cup shredded cabbage
- 1 lime, squeezed

Directions:

1. Make the filling; chop palm hearts into desired pieces.
2. Place the hearts in a bowl along with coconut aminos, chili sauce, and garlic.
3. Cover and refrigerate for 15 minutes.
4. In the meantime, make the hemp seed sauce; place all sauce ingredients into a food blender.
5. Blend until smooth.
6. Heat olive oil in a pan. Add the marinated palm hearts and cook over medium heat for 5 minutes.
7. To assemble; take two lettuce leaves and place in front of you.
8. Add the palm hearts and top with shredded cabbage. Drizzle tacos with hemp seeds sauce and lime juice.
9. Serve immediately.

Nutrition analysis:

- High in vitamin E
- High in thiamin
- High in omega-6

12. Noodles With Pesto

Sea-vegetable noodles with rich and creamy avocado pesto are the perfect lunch option when you simply need something light and refreshing.

Preparation time: 10 minutes + inactive time

Serves: 4

Ingredients:

- 1 package seaweed noodles/kelp noodles
- 2 cups vegetable stock
- 2 tablespoons coconut aminos

For the pesto:

- ½ cup extra-virgin olive oil
- 1 ½ avocados
- 1 cup baby spinach
- 1 pinch red pepper flakes
- ¼ cup fresh basil
- 2 tablespoons almonds
- 2 cloves garlic
- Sea salt and black pepper to taste

Directions:

1. Combine vegetable stock and coconut aminos in a bowl.
2. Add noodles and soak for 30 minutes.
3. In the meantime, make the pesto by combining all the pesto ingredients in a food blender.

4. Blend until smooth.
5. Drain the noodles and place in a wide bowl.
6. Top with avocado pesto and toss to combine.
7. Serve.

Nutrition analysis:
- High in vitamin A
- High in vitamin C

13. "Sausages" With Aioli

Eggplants are a versatile vegetable and can be used for many dishes. Try this version of eggplant "sausages" with creamy garlic aioli. An interesting dish with a great nutritional profile!

Preparation time: 10 minutes + inactive time

Cooking time: 8 minutes

Serves: 6

Ingredients:

Sausages:

- 6 long Japanese eggplants
- ¼ cup olive oil
- 1 teaspoon Italian seasoning
- 1 teaspoon ground fennel seeds
- 2 cloves garlic, minced
- 1 ½ teaspoons kosher salt
- Black pepper, to taste
- Cayenne pepper, to taste

Aioli:

- 4 tablespoons extra-virgin olive oil
- 1 cup silvered almonds
- 2 cloves garlic
- 4 tablespoons lemon juice

- ¼ cup filtered water
- Salt and white pepper, to taste

Extras:

- Keto buns of your choosing

Directions:

1. Make the sausages; peel eggplants using a veggie peeler. Place the eggplants in a zip-lock bag with olive oil, spices, and herbs.
2. Refrigerate eggplants for at least 4 hours or overnight.
3. Heat cast-iron grill pan over medium-high heat. Cook marinated eggplants for 3-4 minutes per side.
4. Make the aioli; place aioli ingredients in a food blender. Blend until smooth for 1 minute.
5. Gradually add water until desired texture is reached. Chill for 30 minutes.
6. To assemble; serve "sausages" with keto-firendly buns, topped with aioli sauce.

Nutrition analysis:

- High in vitamin K
- High in vitamin C
- High in manganese
- Moderate in selenium
- Moderate in phosphorus

14. Cauliflower Salad

Salads cold or warm, are a perfect lunch option. The salads are fairly easy to make, loaded with essential nutrients.

Preparation time: 10 minutes + inactive time

Cooking time: 10 minutes

Serves: 4

Ingredients:

Salad:

- 1 medium head cauliflower
- 1 ½ cups sliced mushrooms, oyster or shiitake
- 1 ½ tablespoons olive oil
- 1 teaspoon fresh dill
- 1 teaspoons chopped chives
- ½ teaspoon smoked paprika
- Salt and pepper, to taste

Sauce:

- ½ cup extra-virgin olive oil
- ¼ cup unsweetened soy milk
- 1 teaspoon raw cider vinegar
- Salt and white pepper, to taste

Directions:

1. Make the salad; cut cauliflower into tiny florets.
2. Place the cauliflower florets into a pan and cover with water.
3. Bring to a boil and reduce heat. Simmer for 3-4 minutes or until crisp tender.
4. In the meantime, heat olive oil in a skillet. Cook mushrooms for 5-8 minutes or until soft. Toss in the cauliflower and shake to coat with oil. Season to taste with salt and pepper.
5. Make the sauce; make sure oil and milk are equal temperatures. It is a very important step.
6. Place soy milk, cider vinegar, and seasonings in a food blender. Blend until smooth. While the blender is running low, gradually stream in extra-virgin olive oil.
7. Blend until thickens.
8. In a bowl, toss cauliflower with prepared sauce, dill, and chives.
9. Divide between bowls and sprinkle with paprika. Chill briefly before serving.

Nutrition analysis:

- High in vitamin C
- High in magnesium
- High in riboflavin

15. Spinach Zucchini Boats

Delicate zucchinis filled with spinach and a vegan alternative to milk-made cheese. If you miss the cheesy consistency, this is for you.

Preparation time: 20 minutes

Cooking time: 20 minutes

Serves: 4

Ingredients:

- 4 zucchinis
- 4 tablespoons blanched almond flour
- 4 tablespoons coconut oil
- 4 tablespoons coconut cream
- 1/8 teaspoon guar gum
- 1 pinch nutmeg
- ¾ cup coconut milk
- 2 cups baby spinach
- Kosher salt and white pepper, to taste

"Cheese":

- ¾ cup almonds
- 3 tablespoons nutritional yeast
- ¼ teaspoon garlic powder

Directions:

1. Heat oven to 400F.
2. Trim zucchinis and cut in half by length. Scoop out the seeds.
3. Place the zucchinis on a baking sheet lined with baking paper. Season with salt and pepper.
4. Heat coconut oil in a skillet. Add almond flour and cook until darkened, to the desired color (go with peanut color).
5. Whisk in coconut milk and nutmeg. Simmer 10 seconds. Add guar gum and stir until thickened.
6. Stir in coconut cream, baby spinach and season with salt. Place aside for 5 minutes.
7. Make the cheese; place all ingredients in a food blender.
8. Blend until coarse mixture is formed. Stir in half the cheese into spinach mixture.
9. Stuff the zucchinis with spinach and sprinkle with nut cheese.
10. Bake 15 minutes or until golden.
11. Serve warm.

Nutrition analysis:

- High in vitamin B
- High in folate
- High in vitamin A
- High in dietary fiber

16. Stuffed Portabella With Nut Pate

The portabella mushroom is a nutritional powerhouse, and should be incorporated into your diet if possible. If you're looking for ways to do so, try out this delicious dish; portabellas stuffed with delicate macadamia nut pate!

Preparation time: 10 minutes

Cooking time: 15 minutes

Serves: 4

Ingredients:

- 4 portabella mushrooms caps, stems removed
- 1 tablespoon olive oil
- 1 tablespoon coconut aminos
- Salt and pepper, to taste

Nut pate:

- 1 cup macadamia nuts, soaked 2 hours
- 1 tablespoon coconut aminos
- 1 celery stalk, chopped
- Kosher salt, to taste

Directions:

1. Heat oven to 375F and line a baking sheet with parchment paper.
2. In a bowl, beat olive oil with coconut aminos. Brush in

mushroom caps with oil mixture and arrange onto a baking sheet.

3. Bake for 15 minutes.
4. In the meantime, make the nut pate; rinse and drain macadamia nuts. Place the macadamia nuts and celery in a food processor and process until just smooth. In the last seconds of processing, add coconut aminos and salt to taste.
5. Process until the coconut aminos is incorporated.
6. Remove the portabella from the oven and place on a plate. Fill with macadamia pate and serve warm.

Nutrition analysis:

- High in vitamin C
- High in riboflavin
- High in niacin
- High in potassium
- Moderate in folate

17. Savory Crepes With Mushroom Cream

Another tasty portabella option, this time creamy, with a nice touch of garlic.

Preparation time: 15 minutes

Cooking time: 15 minutes

Serves: 4
- 2 tablespoons coconut flour
- 1 1/3 cups almond milk
- 4 tablespoons coconut oil
- 2 tablespoons flax seeds + 2/3 cup water

Mushroom cream:
- 8 portabella mushrooms, caps only
- ¼ cup olive oil
- ½ cup macadamia nuts soaked 4 hours
- 2 sprigs fresh thyme
- 2 tablespoons coconut cream
- 4 cloves garlic, unpeeled
- Salt and white pepper, to taste

Directions:
1. Make the crepes; in a food blender, blend all ingredients.
2. Let the batter rest for 15 minutes.
3. Heat a large non-stick skillet over medium heat. Pour ¼ cup batter into skillet and swirl to distribute the batter evenly over the skillet bottom.

4. Cook until bubbles appear and carefully fill the crepe to another side.
5. Cook for 1 minute. Repeat with remaining batter. Keep pancakes warm.
6. Heat oven to 375F and grease baking sheet with some cooking spray.
7. Place the mushrooms onto a baking sheet and season with salt.
8. In a food blender, process olive oil, garlic, and thyme. Brush each mushroom with prepared mixture and bake for 15 minutes.
9. Transfer the mushrooms to a food blender. Drain and rinse macadamia nuts and place in a food blender with mushrooms. Blend until desired consistency is reached.
10. Spread the pate over crepes and roll or fold gently.
11. Serve immediately.

Nutrition analysis:
- High in riboflavin
- High in niacin
- High in potassium
- Moderate in folate

18. Crust-Less Quiche

A wonderful combination of asparagus, kale, and a nut-based creamy filling — all combined in a crust-less quiche.

Preparation time: 15 minutes

Cooking time: 30 minutes

Serves: 4-6

Ingredients:

-   4 tablespoons coconut oil
-   2 cups asparagus, trimmed and chopped
-   2 cups kale
-   8oz. sliced oyster mushrooms
-   1 garlic clove, minced
-   Salt and pepper, to taste

Filling:

-   1 cup Brazil nuts, soaked 4 hours
-   ¼ cup nutritional yeast
-   1 ¾ cup full-fat coconut milk
-   1/3 cup softened coconut butter
-   ½ cup almond flour
-   3 tablespoons lemon juice
-   1 teaspoon turmeric powder
-   Salt and pepper, to taste

Directions:

1. Heat coconut oil in a skillet. Add sliced mushrooms, minced garlic, and cook 6 minutes.
2. Toss in kale and asparagus and cook 3-4 minutes, Season to taste.
3. Remove from heat and place aside.
4. Make the filling; rinse and drain Brazil nuts. Place in a food processor with coconut milk and process until creamy.
5. Add remaining ingredients and process until smooth.
6. Transfer into a bowl, and stir in kale-mushroom mixture.
7. Heat oven to 350F. Pour mixture into 9-inch pie pan and bake 30 minutes or until firm to the touch.
8. Cool 20 minutes before slicing and serving.

Nutrition analysis:

- High in manganese
- High in vitamin B
- High in folate

19. Veggie Fritters With Avocado

Fritters are not reserved only for breakfast. These fritters will satisfy even the most demanding gourmet lover, while keeping them full and healthy.

Preparation time: 10 minutes

Cooking time: 10 minutes

Serves: 4

Ingredients:

- 1 large zucchini
- 2 portabella mushrooms
- 1 tablespoon ground flax seeds + 3 tablespoons water
- ¼ cup almond meal
- 1 cup packed chopped spinach
- 1 avocado
- ¼ cup macadamia nuts soaked 4 hours
- 1 tablespoon raw hemp seeds
- 1 teaspoon dried basil
- Salt and pepper, to taste
- 2-3 tablespoons olive oil, for frying

Sauce:

- ½ cup silvered almonds, soaked 4 hours
- 3 tablespoons extra-virgin olive oil
- 1 clove garlic
- ½ teaspoon chili powder

- ¼ cup filtered water
- 2 tablespoons lemon juice
- Salt, to taste

Directions:

1. Make the fritters; combine flax seeds and water in a small bowl. Place aside for 10 minutes.
2. Shred zucchinis and mushrooms. Squeeze to remove excess liquid and place in a bowl.
3. Rinse and drain macadamia and process in a food blender with hemp seeds until creamy.
4. Add the macadamia cream and flax mixture into a bowl with zucchinis.
5. Add the chopped spinach and stir to combine.
6. Heat half the oil in a pan. Scoop fritters into the pan and cook 2 minutes per side.
7. Repeat with remaining oil and batter.
8. Make sauce; drain and rinse soaked almonds. Place in a food blender with remaining ingredients, except extra-virgin olive oil. Blend until smooth. While the blender is running low, stream in the olive oil and blend until emulsified.
9. Serve fritters with sauce.

Nutrition analysis:

- High in vitamin A
- High in vitamin K

20. Creamy Cauliflower Soup

Rich, creamy, and aromatic soup. Super healthy, and very easy to make.

Preparation time: 10 minutes

Cooking time: 15 minutes

Serves: 4

Ingredients:

- 2 cups cauliflower florets
- 2 cups sliced wild mushrooms
- 2 cups full-fat coconut milk
- 2 tablespoons avocado oil
- 1 teaspoon dried celery flakes
- ½ tablespoons fresh chopped thyme
- 1 clove garlic, minced
- Salt and pepper, to taste

Directions:

1. In a saucepan, combine cauliflower, coconut milk, and celery flakes.
2. Cover and bring to a boil over medium-high heat.
3. Reduce heat and simmer for 6-7 minutes. Remove from the heat and puree using an immersion blender.
4. In the meantime, heat avocado oil in a skillet. Add garlic and thyme and cook until fragrant. Toss in wild mushrooms and cook for 6-7 minutes or until tender.

5. Pour in pureed cauliflower and bring to a boil. Reduce heat and simmer 6-8 minutes or until thickened.
6. Serve warm with Keto bread.

Nutrition analysis:
- High in manganese
- High in niacin

Dinner Recipes

21. Keto Vegan Falafel

Falafel is usually made with chickpeas or fava beans. However, since we're shooting for low-carb we decided to go with some other ingredients. If you love a classic falafel, try this.

Preparation time: 10 minutes

Cooking time: 10 minutes

Serves: 4-6

Ingredients:
- ½ cup raw hemp hearts
- 1 tablespoon chopped cilantro
- 1 tablespoon chopped basil
- 2 cloves garlic, minced
- ½ teaspoon ground cumin seeds
- ½ teaspoon chili powder
- 1 tablespoon flax meal + 2 tablespoons filtered water
- Sea salt and pepper, to taste
- Avocado or coconut oil, to fry

Sauce:

- ½ cup tahini
- ¼ cup fresh lime juice
- ½ cup filtered water
- 2 tablespoons extra-virgin olive oil
- Sea salt, to taste
- A good pinch ground cumin seeds

Directions:

1. Mix flax with filtered water in a small bowl.
2. Place aside for 10 minutes.
3. In meantime, combine raw hemp hearts, cilantro, basil, garlic, cumin, chili, and seasonings in a food processor.
4. Process until just comes together. Add the flax seeds mixture and process until finely blended and uniform.
5. Heat approximately 2 tablespoons avocado oil in a skillet. Shape 1 tablespoon mixture into balls and fry for 3-4 minutes or until deep golden brown.
6. Remove from the skillet and place on a plate lined with paper towels.
7. Make the sauce; combine all ingredients in a food blender. Blend until smooth and creamy.
8. Serve falafel with fresh lettuce salad and tahini sauce.

Nutrition analysis:

- High in manganese
- High in copper
- Moderate in phosphorus

22. Italian Baked Mushrooms

Delicious tender mushrooms made with Italian herbs, extra-virgin olive oil, and some super-fast creamy nut cheese.

Preparation time: 10 minutes

Cooking time: 25 minutes

Serves: 4

Ingredients:

- 1lb. sliced portabella mushrooms, caps only
- 4 green bell peppers, sliced
- 4 tablespoons olive oil
- 1 tablespoon extra-virgin olive oil
- 2 tablespoons fresh chopped basil
- 1 teaspoon dried oregano
- Salt and pepper, to taste

Topping:

- 1 cup macadamia nuts
- 4 tablespoons nutritional yeast
- ½ teaspoon dried garlic
- Salt, to taste

Directions:

1. Heat oven to 400F.
2. Cut bell peppers in half, remove seeds and place on a baking

sheet. Drizzle the peppers with 1 tablespoon olive oil and sprinkle with black pepper.
3. Roast 25 minutes or until slightly charred. Transfer into the clean zip-lock bag and allow to cool completely. Peel off the skin and place the peppers with some salt, extra-virgin olive oil, and basil in a food blender.
4. Blend until smooth.
5. Heat remaining olive oil in a skillet. Add oregano and cook until fragrant. Toss in the mushrooms and cook for 8 minutes.
6. Make the topping; in a food processor process, the topping ingredients until a fine meal is formed.
7. Transfer the mushrooms into baking dish. Top with green bell pepper sauce and macadamia nut topping.
8. Bake 20 minutes in the heated oven at 400F.
9. Serve warm.

Nutrition analysis:
-   High in vitamin B
-   High in folate

23. Avocado & Spinach Gazpacho

Cold gazpacho soup you can make in advance and serve whenever you want. It is a perfect option for a summer dinner, and is best served with some keto-firendly bread croutons.

Preparation time: 10 minutes

Serves: 4-6

Ingredients:

- 1 ½ avocado, peeled, chopped
- 2 medium cucumbers, peeled and chopped
- 1 handful baby spinach
- 2 stalks celery
- 2 tablespoons extra-virgin olive oil
- ½ jalapeno pepper, seeded
- 2 cup cold homemade vegetable stock or water
- 1/3 cup loosely packed cilantro
- 2 cloves garlic, minced
- 2 limes, juiced
- 1 teaspoon ground fennel seeds
- Sea salt and pepper, to taste

Directions:

1. In a food processor, process cucumbers and celery, and place in a large bowl. (you can also use a food blender)
2. Process celery, jalapeno and garlic, and place in a bowl.
3. Next, process spinach and basil, and place in a bowl.
4. Pour in 2 cups water or vegetable stock and process until smooth. Pour into a bowl, reserving 2 cups mixture.

5. Add in remaining ingredients and process until smooth. Pour into a bowl, and stir to combine.
6. Chill for few hours before serving.

Nutrition analysis:
- High in vitamin K
- High in vitamin E
- High in calcium

24. Healthy Green Tabbouleh

This Ketogenic version of well-known Eastern salad will surprise you with its easy preparation and outstanding flavor.

Preparation time: 10 minutes

Cooking time: 5 minutes

Serves: 4

Ingredients:

- 3 cups "riced" cauliflower
- 3 tablespoons extra-virgin coconut oil
- 1 avocado, peeled, cubed
- 2 large cucumber, peeled and diced
- 3 cups spinach, chopped
- ½ cup fresh lemon juice
- ½ cup extra-virgin olive oil
- ½ cup fresh chopped parsley
- ½ cup fresh chopped mint
- 1 clove garlic, minced
- 1 spring onion (optional) chopped
- Salt and pepper, to taste

Directions:
1. Heat coconut oil in a skillet.
2. Add cauliflower and cook over medium heat for 5 minutes or until crisp tender.
3. Remove from heat and place aside.

4. Prepare the remaining ingredients, as described.
5. Place the chopped vegetables in a bowl. Top with chopped herbs and cauliflower.
6. In a small bowl, whisk lemon juice, olive oil, and minced garlic.
7. Pour over tabbouleh and toss to combine.
8. Chill briefly before serving.

Nutrition analysis:

- High in vitamin C
- High in vitamin A

25. Olive Cauliflower Non-Meatballs

Vegetable "meatballs" are often not the healthiest option, as they sacrifice nutrition in order to resemble actual meat as closely as possible.

However, these little beauties, made largely from cauliflower, are loaded with quality ingredients that your body will appreciate.

Preparation time: 10 minutes

Cooking time: 25 minutes

Serves: 4

Ingredients:
- 2 cups cauliflower florets
- ½ cup sprouted mung beans
- 1 tablespoon ground flax seeds
- 2 tablespoons extra-virgin coconut oil
- ½ cup chopped green olives
- 1 clove garlic, minced
- ¼ cup chopped fresh parsley
- ½ teaspoon red chili flakes
- 1 teaspoon dried oregano
- Salt and pepper, to taste

Chutney:

- ¼ cup mint
- ¼ cup coriander
- ½ juiced lemon
- 1 green chili
- ½ cup unsweetened grated coconut
- Salt, to taste

Directions:

1. Place the sprouted mung beans in a pan. Cover with water and simmer for 25-30 minutes.
2. In the last 5 minutes of cooking toss in the cauliflower florets and cook until crisp tender.
3. Place in a colander to drain completely.
4. Transfer in a food blender and blend until smooth.
5. Add olives, garlic, parsley, chili flakes, oregano, salt, and pepper. Combine flax seeds with 2 tablespoons water and place aside to gel.
6. Stir the "flax egg" into the cauliflower mixture and stir all to combine.
7. Shape the mixture into 1 ½ -inch balls and arrange on baking sheet lined with parchment paper.
8. Bake 20 minutes, flip and cook for 5 minutes more.
9. Make the chutney: place all ingredients in a food processor. Process until smooth.
10. Serve meatballs with chutney.

Nutrition analysis:
- High in vitamin K
- High in vitamin A

26. Veggie Pizza Deluxe

A vegan, ketogenic pizza? Yes, it's real. This pizza is made with spinach pesto and topped with some healthy veggies. You can choose your own topping ingredients to suit your personal tastes, of course.

Preparation time: 15 minutes

Cooking time: 15 minutes

Serves: 6

Ingredients:

Crust:

-   1 cup almond flour
-   ¼ cup sifted coconut flour
-   1 teaspoon kosher salt
-   ¾ cup ground flax seeds
-   2 tablespoons ground white chia seeds
-   1 tablespoon psyllium husks powder
-   1 cup water

Pesto:

-   ½ cup macadamia nuts
-   1 cup baby spinach
-   1 clove garlic
-   ½ cup nutritional yeast

- ½ cup avocado oil
- 2 tablespoons lemon juice
- Salt, to taste

Topping:

- 2 tablespoons olive oil
- 1 cup baby Bella mushrooms, sliced
- 1 green bell pepper, sliced
- ½ cup broccoli florets
- Fresh basil, chopped

Directions:

1. Make the crust; combine all crust ingredients in a bowl.
2. Knead until smooth. Cover and place aside for 20 minutes.
3. Roll the dough between two pieces of baking paper to ¼-inch thick. With fingers roll the ends to create a rim that will hold pesto. Transfer the pizza onto a baking sheet lined with parchment paper and bake 10 minutes at 375F.
4. Make the pesto; in a food blender, combine pesto ingredients. Blend until smooth.
5. Make the topping; heat oven to 400F. Spread bell pepper and broccoli onto a baking sheet. Drizzle with oil and season to taste. Roast 10 minutes.
6. Assemble pizza; spread pesto over pizza crust. Top with roasted veggies and mushrooms. Bake 5-6 minutes at 375F. Serve warm.

Nutrition analysis:

- High in vitamin K
- Moderate in protein

27. Creamy "Cauli Rice" With Spinach

Sauteed spinach with rice makes a light, healthy, and delicious dinner meal.

Preparation time: 5 minutes

Cooking time: 7 minutes

Serves: 4

Ingredients:
- 3 cups "riced" cauliflower
- 1 ½ cups packed baby spinach
- 1 tablespoon avocado oil
- 2 tablespoons coconut aminos
- 1 teaspoon dried garlic
- ¼ cup macadamia nuts, soaked 4 hours
- 1 tablespoon nutritional yeast
- Salt, to taste

Directions:
1. Heat avocado oil in a skillet.
2. Add cauliflower and cook 3-4 minutes, stirring. Stir in coconut aminos.
3. In the meantime, rinse macadamia and place in a food blender along with garlic and nutritional yeast.
4. Add spinach to cauliflower and cook until wilted.
5. Pour over macadamia mix and cook for 5 minutes.
6. Serve.

Nutrition analysis:
- High in magnesium
- High in thiamin
- Moderate in protein

28. Eggplant & Zucchini Stack

Zucchini fritters with eggplants as low-carb buns, with a creamy avocado sour cream.

Preparation time: 10 minutes

Cooking time: 10 minutes

Serves: 4

Ingredients:

Zucchini fritters:

- 2 cups grated zucchinis
- ¼ cup fresh parsley, chopped
- 2 tablespoons coconut flour
- 1 tablespoon ground flax seeds + 2 tablespoons water
- 1 tablespoon coconut oil
- Salt and pepper, to taste

Eggplant:

- 1 large eggplant, sliced into ¼- inch thick round
- 1 tablespoon coconut oil

Avocado cream:

- 1 avocado, pitted, peeled
- ¼ cup full-fat coconut milk

- 2 tablespoons extra-virgin olive or coconut oil
- 1 tablespoon fresh lime juice
- Salt, to taste

Directions:

1. Make the fritters; place grated zucchinis in a colander and sprinkle with some salt. Leave to drain 10 minutes. Squeeze out liquid as much as possible.
2. In a bowl, combine flax seeds and water. Place aside until gel.
3. Stir in the zucchinis and remaining fritter ingredients, except oil. Heat oil in a skillet.
4. Shape 2 tablespoons zucchini mixture into balls and flatten each gently.
5. Fry the fritters for 3 minutes per side.
6. Prepare the eggplant; season sliced eggplant with salt and place in a colander for 30 minutes. Rinse and pat-dry. Heat grill pan over medium-high heat. Add oil and once hot, grill the eggplant for 3 minutes per side. Place aside and keep warm.
7. Make the sauce; in a food blender, combine all sauce ingredients. Blend until smooth and creamy.
8. To serve; place an eggplant slice in front of you. Top with avocado sauce and sandwich with remaining eggplant slices. You can also add some salad. Serve.

Nutrition analysis:
- High in vitamin K
- High in vitamin C
- High in folate
- High in dietary fiber

29. Eggplant Fingers With Macadamia Hummus

Crispy vegetable fingers served with macadamia-based hummus. This is a perfect dish to serve for dinner parties. It is easy to digest, while being rich in healthy fats.

Preparation time: 10 minutes

Cooking time: 45 minutes

Serves: 4

Ingredients:

Eggplant bites:

- 1 medium diced eggplant
- 4 cloves garlic, unpeeled
- 1 tablespoon extra-virgin avocado oil
- 1 cup fine almond flour
- 1 tablespoon flax seeds + 2 tablespoons water
- 1 teaspoon dried basil

Hummus:

- ½ cup macadamia nuts
- 1 clove garlic
- 1 tablespoon water
- 1 tablespoon tahini
- 1 tablespoon coconut oil

- 1 ½ tablespoons fresh lemon juice
- Salt and pepper, to taste

Directions:

1. Make the fingers; combine flax seeds with water in a bowl. Place aside for 10 minutes.
2. Heat oven to 400F and line baking tray with parchment paper.
3. Place eggplants and garlic onto a baking tray and toss with olive oil, salt, and pepper.
4. Roast for 40 minutes. Remove and place aside to cool.
5. Transfer cooled eggplant into a food processor and squeeze garlic from the peel. Add remaining ingredients, including flax seeds and pulse until just combined.
6. Shape the mixture into fingers and arrange on a baking sheet lined with parchment paper.
7. Bake the fingers for 45 minutes, turning halfway through baking.
8. Make the hummus; combine the hummus ingredients in a food processor. Process until smooth.
9. Serve hummus with eggplant fingers.

Nutrition analysis:

- High in thiamin
- High in manganese

30. Tofu Salad

Sometimes you have to try something new, and this salad is all about new and exciting flavors; marinated tofu served with Bok Choy and chili sambal dressing!

Preparation time: 15 minutes

Cooking time: 30 minutes

Serves: 4

Ingredients:

- 15oz. extra firm drained tofu
- 1 tablespoon coconut aminos
- 1 tablespoon coconut oil
- 2 teaspoons minced garlic
- 1 tablespoon filtered water
- ½ lemon juice

For the salad:

- 9oz. fresh Bok Choy
- 3 tablespoons extra-virgin coconut oil
- 2 tablespoons coconut aminos
- 2 tablespoons chopped parsley
- 1 tablespoon almond butter
- 1 tablespoon ground chili sambal

Directions:

1. Make the tofu; cut tofu into squares and place in a bowl.
2. In a small bowl, whisk coconut aminos, coconut oil, garlic, water, and lemon juice. Pour mixture over tofu and toss gently to combine. Cover and refrigerate 1 hour.
3. Heat oven to 350F and line a baking sheet with parchment paper. Arrange the tofu on a baking sheet and bake 30 minutes.
4. Make the Bok choy; in a bowl, combine all ingredients except Bok choy and lemon juice.
5. Just before tofu is baked, stir in lemon juice. Chop the Bok choy and stir into prepared dressing.
6. Remove tofu cubes from oven and serve with Bok choy.

Nutrition analysis:

- High in protein
- High in manganese

Snacks

31. Avocado Slices

For obvious reasons, fries are not a keto-friendly food. Instead, try out these avocado slices, best served with creamy chili dip.

Preparation time: 5 minutes

Cooking time: 1 minutes

Serves: 2

Ingredients:
- 2 ripe avocados
- ¼ cup whipped coconut cream
- 1 cup almond meal
- 1 cup olive oil
- 1 pinch cayenne pepper
- Salt, to taste

Chili dip:
- 1 cup extra-virgin olive oil
- ½ cup almond milk
- 2 teaspoons cider vinegar
- 1 teaspoon chili powder
- Salt, to taste

Directions:

1. Peel, pit, and slice avocados.
2. Place whipped coconut cream in a small bowl.
3. In a separate bowl, combine almond meal with salt and cayenne pepper.
4. Heat oil in a deep pan.
5. Place avocado pieces into heated oil and fry 45 seconds.
6. Transfer to a paper lined plate.
7. Make a chili dip; blend all dip ingredients, except the oil in a food blender until smooth. Stream in oil and blend until creamy. Serve with avocado slices.

Nutrition analysis:

- High in vitamin E
- High in omega-3
- High in omega 6

32. Kale Chips With Dip

Tasty kale chips – not soggy or burned, but perfectly seasoned and baked kale chips. They are crunchy, highly addictive and great for the entire family.

Preparation time: 10 minutes

Cooking time: 12 minutes

Serves: 4

Ingredients:

- 1 bunch kale, torn into medium-sized pieces
- 2 tablespoons olive oil
- Salt, to taste
- Dried herbs or spices (basil, cayenne, chili) - optional

Dip:

- ½ cup avocado oil
- ¼ cup soy milk
- 1 clove garlic
- 2 tablespoons chopped parsley
- 1 teaspoon cider vinegar
- ¼ teaspoon chili powder
- Salt and white pepper, to taste

Directions:

1. Wash the kale, separate the leaves and stem and place onto kitchen towels to drain.
2. Torn kale into medium-sized pieces and place in a zip-lock bag with olive oil, salt, and desired seasoning.
3. Shake until each kale leaf is coated.
4. Heat oven to 350F and line two baking sheets with parchment paper.
5. Arrange the kale leaves onto baking sheets and bake 12 minutes.
6. In the meantime, make the dip; place ingredients in a jar or jug. Blend using an immersion blender until emulsified and smooth.
7. Serve kale chips with freshly prepared dip.

Nutrition analysis:

- High in vitamin E
- High in vitamin K
- Moderate in protein
- Moderate in phosphorus

33. Almond Butter With Celery Sticks

Healthy snacks don't have to be difficult to make, and this recipe is a proof of it.

Preparation time: 25 minutes

Cooking time: 25 minutes

Serves: 4

Ingredients:
- 1 cup almonds
- ½ lb. celery sticks
- 1 pinch sea salt

Directions:
1. Heat oven to 250F and spread almonds onto a baking sheet.
2. Bake the almonds 25 minutes, stirring halfway through baking.
3. Transfer the almonds to a food processor. Add sea salt.
4. Process the almonds until smooth and creamy, stopping as needed to scrape down the blender sides. It takes around 25 minutes.
5. In the meantime, trim the celery and remove leaves.
6. Serve almond butter with celery.

Nutrition analysis:
- High in riboflavin
- High in dietary fiber
- High in vitamin K
- Moderate in vitamin E

34. Palm Fingers

Palm hearts have a very mild flavor. As they are very easy to prepare, they are the perfect option when you need some quick snacks.

Preparation time: 5 minutes

Cooking time: 5 minutes

Serves: 4

Ingredients:

- 2 14oz. can palm hearts, rinsed, cut into quarters
- 2 cups almond flour
- 1 cup whipped coconut cream
- 1 teaspoon Italian seasoning
- 1 teaspoon chili powder
- Salt, to taste
- Coconut oil, for frying

Dip:

- ½ cup raw hemp seeds
- ¼ cup avocado oil
- 4 tablespoons cashew milk
- 2 teaspoons fresh dill
- ¼ teaspoon dried garlic flakes
- 4 tablespoons water
- Salt and pepper, to taste

Directions:

1. Make the palm fingers; let the oil heat in a skillet.
2. In a small bowl, combine whipped coconut cream, and chili powder.
3. In a separate bowl, combine almond flour, Italian seasoning, some salt, and pepper.
4. Dip palm fingers into coconut cream and dredge through almond flour. Fry the palm hearts in heated oil for 2-3 minutes or until golden-brown.
5. Make the sauce; in a food blender, combine all ingredients, except the oil. Blend until smooth. While the blender is running low, stream in avocado oil. Blend until emulsified.
6. Serve palm fingers with prepared dip.

Nutrition analysis:

- High in copper
- High in zinc
- High in vitamin B6

35. Avocado Mushroom Bombs

An irresistible, creamy, protein-rich and easy to make ketogenic-vegan snack.

Preparation time: 10 minutes + inactive time

Serves: 6

Ingredients:
- ½ large avocado
- ¼ cup coconut oil (not melted)
- 1 clove garlic, minced
- 1 chili pepper, seeded, chopped
- 2 tablespoons fresh chopped cilantro
- ½ tablespoon lime juice
- 1 cup sliced mushrooms
- 1 teaspoon olive oil
- Salt, to taste

Directions:
1. Heat olive oil in a skillet. Add mushrooms and cook for 6-8 minutes or until tender.
2. Place aside.
3. In a bowl, mash the avocado with coconut oil, garlic, chili pepper, cilantro, lime juice, and some salt.
4. Stir in the mushrooms and cover with a clean foil. Refrigerate 30 minutes.
5. Shape the mixture into 6 balls with an ice-cream scoop.
6. Serve immediately.

NOTE: You can also roll the balls through almond meal.

Nutrition analysis:

- High in vitamin E
- Moderate in phosphorus

36. Ketogenic Tofu Bites

Tofu bites are rich in fiber, protein, and charged with an arsenal of health benefits. Tofu has a bland taste, but with simple ingredients you can turn it into an outstanding snack.

Preparation time: 5 minutes

Cooking time: 5 minutes

Serves: 4

Ingredients:

- 1 package extra-firm tofu, drained
- 2 tablespoons sliced almonds
- 1 tablespoon white sesame seeds
- 1 tablespoon coconut oil
- 1 teaspoon walnut oil
- ¼ teaspoon dried garlic flakes
- 2 tablespoons coconut aminos
- ½ teaspoon red chili flakes
- 2 tablespoons filtered water
- Salt and pepper, to taste

Directions:

1. Cut tofu into 1-inch cubes.
2. Heat coconut oil in a skillet. Add tofu and cook for 2 minutes per side.
3. Add almonds and cook for 1 minute.
4. Add all the remaining ingredients and cook until sauce is

reduced.
5. Serve with desired veggies.

Nutrition analysis:

- High in protein
- High in omega 3
- High in calcium

37. Zucchini Rolls With Nut Butter

Healthy, easy to make, and done in no time...what else to look for.

Preparation time: 10 minutes

Cooking time: 2 minutes

Serves: 4

Ingredients:

- 3 medium zucchinis, trimmed
- 2 tablespoons olive oil
- Salt and pepper, to taste

Nut butter:

- 1 cup Brazil nuts
- 1 good pinch salt

Extras:

- 1 cup steamed and chopped broccoli

Directions:

1. Heat grill pan over medium-high heat.
2. Slice the zucchinis by a length to ¼-inch thick.
3. Brush the zucchini slices with olive oil on both sides and season with salt to taste.

4. Grill the zucchini slices for 4 minutes per side.
5. In the meantime, make nut butter. Toast Brazil nuts 2-3 minutes in a dry skillet over medium heat.
6. Leave the nuts to cool. Once cooled transfer into a food processor with a pinch of salt.
7. Process until you have a creamy and smooth mixture.
8. Spread nut butter over zucchini slices. Top with some broccoli and roll gently.
9. Serve immediately.

Nutrition analysis:

- High in selenium
- High in omega-6
- Moderate in vitamin A
- Moderate in protein

38. Fried Guacamole

These little guacamole balls are a very unique and tasty snack. You can serve with a favorite dip or some fresh salad.

Preparation time: 10 minutes + inactive time

Cooking time: 5 minutes

Serves: 4

Ingredients:

- 2 ripe avocados
- 1 Jalapeno pepper, seeded, chopped
- ¼ cup almond meal
- 1 teaspoon chili powder
- 1 tablespoon fresh lime juice
- ½ teaspoon ground cumin
- Salt, to taste
- Coconut oil, for frying

Coating:

- ¼ cup ground flax seeds
- 2 tablespoons almond flour
- ½ teaspoon ground mustard seeds

Directions:

1. In a bowl, mash avocados. Add remaining ingredients and stir to combine.

2. Shape the mixture into walnut size balls and place in a freezer for 10 minutes just to harden.
3. In a wide plate combine flax seeds, almond flour, and ground mustard seeds.
4. Heat 2-inches coconut oil in a skillet.
5. Dredge guacamole balls through the almond mixture and drop carefully into heated oil.
6. Fry for 2-3 minutes or until golden.
7. Serve while still hot.

Nutrition analysis:
- High in vitamin A
- High in dietary fiber
- High in omega 3
- High in omega 6

39. Green Smoothie

This smoothie is made with fresh ingredients, and are packed with vitamins, minerals, proteins, and even healthy fats. We are sure you will love this emerald green ketogenic-vegan smoothie.

Preparation time: 2 minutes

Serves: 1

Ingredients:

- 1 cup almond milk
- 1 ½ cups spinach
- 2 tablespoons MTC oil
- 4-6 ice cubes
- Few drops Stevia, to taste
- 1 large cucumber, peeled

Directions:

1. Combine all ingredients in a food blender.
2. Blend until smooth.
3. Serve immediately.

Nutrition analysis:

- High in protein
- High in vitamin A
- High in vitamin C
- High in dietary fiber

40. Icy Pops

Avocado Popsicles made with a coconut milk, almond butter, and a hint of vanilla. They are creamy, rich, and everything you need from a frozen treat.

Preparation time: 5 minutes + inactive time

Serves: 4

Ingredients:

- 1 avocado, pitted, peeled
- 1 ½ teaspoons vanilla paste
- 1 cup coconut milk
- 2 tablespoons almond butter
- Few drops stevia, to taste
- ¼ teaspoon Ceylon cinnamon

Directions:

1. Combine all ingredients in a food blender.
2. Blend until smooth.
3. Transfer the mixture into popsicle molds and insert popsicle sticks.
4. Freeze 4 hours or until firm.
5. Serve.

Nutrition analysis:

- High in dietary fiber
- High in vitamin E
- Moderate in copper

Desserts

41. Almond butter balls

Tasty bites with carob powder and rich almond butter. If you do not like carob, use raw cocoa powder instead.

Preparation time: 10 minutes + inactive time

Serves: 14 balls

Ingredients:

- 3 tablespoons almond butter
- 3 tablespoons carob powder
- 3 teaspoons almond flour
- 2 teaspoons powdered Erythritol or Yacon powder
- ½ cup unsweetened coconut flakes

Directions:
1. In a bowl, combine almond butter, carob powder, almond flour, and Erythritol.
2. Stir until combined.
3. Place coconut flakes in a small bowl.
4. Scoop prepared a mixture with a small ice cream scoop and drop into coconut flakes.
5. Roll until completely covered with the coconut flakes. Arrange the balls on a plate and refrigerate for 4-6 hour or until firm.
6. Serve and enjoy.

Nutrition analysis:

- High in riboflavin
- High in calcium
- High in potassium

42. Cocoa Pumpkin Fudge

Creamy, smooth, melt-in-your-mouth fudge is a healthy dessert you can freely consume without feeling any guilt.

Preparation time: 10 minutes + inactive time

Serves: 24 slices

Ingredients:

- 1 cup organic unsweetened pumpkin puree
- 1 ¾ cups cocoa butter
- 1 teaspoon allspice
- 1 tablespoon melted coconut oil

Directions:

1. Line 8-inch glass dish with baking paper.
2. Melt cocoa butter over medium heat.
3. Stir in pumpkin puree and allspice. Stir to combine.
4. Add coconut oil and stir well. Transfer the mixture into a prepared glass dish and press down to distribute evenly.
5. Cover with a second piece of baking paper and refrigerate 2 hours.
6. Slice and serve.

Nutrition analysis:

- High in manganese
- High in saturated fat
- High in vitamin K
- High in vitamin E

43. Coconut Vanilla Panna Cotta

A quick dessert you can always make in no time with only few ingredients. You will love its flavor and smooth texture.

Preparation time: 5 minutes + inactive time

Cooking time: 5 minutes

Serves: 6

Ingredients:

- 14oz. can full-fat coconut milk
- 1 tablespoon melted coconut oil
- 1 scoop vanilla flavored hemp seed protein powder
- 1 ½ teaspoons agar-agar powder
- ¼ cup shredded toasted coconut

Directions:

1. In a food blender, blend coconut milk, coconut oil, and protein powder.
2. Pour the mixture into the saucepan and stir in agar-agar powder.
3. Bring the mixture to a gentle simmer. Cook until agar-agar is completely dissolved and the mixture is thickened.
4. Grease 6 ramekins with coconut oil and pour in panna cotta.
5. Chill in the fridge for 2 hours.
6. Serve, garnished with toasted coconut.

Nutrition analysis:

- High in dietary fiber
- High in protein
- High in manganese

44. Creamy Vanilla Custard

Light, creamy, and vanilla-flavored custard, made with macadamia nut butter.

Preparation time: 5 minutes

Cooking time: 5 minutes

Serves: 4

Ingredients:

- 1 cup full-fat coconut milk
- ½ cup coconut cream
- 1/3 cup macadamia nut butter
- 1/3 cup Yacon powder
- 1 teaspoon vanilla paste
- 1 teaspoon agar-agar powder

Directions:

1. Heat coconut milk in a saucepan.
2. Stir in macadamia nut butter, Yacon powder, and agar-agar.
3. Simmer gently until starts to thicken.
4. Stir in coconut cream and vanilla paste.
5. Divide mixture between four ramekins.
6. Chill in a fridge until set. Serve and enjoy.

Nutrition analysis:
- High in thiamin
- High in manganese

45. Nutty Brownies

No-fuss recipe, suitable for ketogenic-vegan diet followers, made with raw cocoa powder and macadamia nuts.

Preparation time: 10 minutes

Cooking time: 25 minutes

Serves: 9

Ingredients:
- ¾ cup macadamia nuts
- ¾ cup almond flour
- ¾ cup Yacon powder
- ¼ cup coconut oil
- 4 tablespoons cocoa butter
- 1 scoop chocolate flavored hemp seed protein powder
- 1 teaspoon vanilla extract
- 3 tablespoons raw cocoa powder
- 2 tablespoons flax seeds + ¼ cup water

Directions:
1. Heat oven to 350F and line 8-inch baking dish with a parchment paper.
2. In a small bowl, combine flax seeds with water. Place aside 10 minutes.
3. In a bowl, cream together Yacon powder, coconut oil, and cocoa butter.
4. Fold in the flax mixture and vanilla.

5. Add remaining ingredients, except the macadamia nuts.
6. Once you have a creamy batter, fold in the macadamia nuts.
7. Spread the batter into prepared baking dish and bake 25 minutes.
8. Remove the brownies from the oven and place aside to cool.
9. Slice before serving.

Nutrition analysis:

- High in dietary fiber
- High in vitamin E
- High in saturated fat

46. Refreshing "Fat Bombs"

Some may think the word "fat bomb" sounds negative, but this recipe is actually delicious and healthy — not all fat is bad! With only few ingredients you can enjoy these refreshing lime-coconut fat bombs.

Preparation time: 10 minutes + inactive time

Serves: 8

Ingredients:

- 1 ½ teaspoons lime zest
- 1 tablespoon lime juice
- ¼ cup cocoa butter
- ¼ cup melted coconut oil
- Few drops stevia, to taste

Directions:
1. Prepare 8 silicone muffin cups.
2. Melt cocoa butter and coconut oil over a double boiler.
3. Sri in lime zest and lime juice, along with the desired amount of stevia.
4. Pour into silicone molds and place in the fridge.
5. Chill until hardened.
6. Remove from the molds and serve.

Nutrition analysis:

- High in vitamin C
- High in vitamin E
- High in vitamin K

47. Chocolate Hemp Mousse

Raw cocoa powder and coffee are the main stars of this creamy and rich dessert. If you need something airy, smooth, and elegant to treat your friends to, or to simply pamper yourself, then prepare this amazing mousse.

Preparation time: 10 minutes + inactive time

Serves: 4

Ingredients:

- 2 cups coconut cream
- 2 scoops cocoa flavored hemp protein powder
- ¼ cup chia seeds
- 7 drops stevia
- 1 teaspoon instant coffee
- Raw cocoa nibs, to sprinkle (optional)

Directions:

1. Place all ingredients in a large mixing bowl.
2. Whisk the ingredients until smooth.
3. Divide mixture between 4 dessert glasses.
4. Chill in a fridge for 3 hours.
5. Serve sprinkled with cocoa nibs.

Nutrition analysis:

- High in Omega-6
- Moderate in calcium
- Moderate in phosphorus

48. Peanut Butter Cookies

These keto-friendly cookies has an enjoyable, smooth peanut butter flavor, with a protein boost from the hemp protein powder.

Preparation time: 10 minutes

Cooking time: 10 minutes

Serves: 12

Ingredients:

- 1 cup smooth peanut butter
- ¾ cup almond flour
- ½ cup powdered Erythritol
- ¼ cup almond milk
- 1 scoop vanilla flavored hemp protein powder
- 1 teaspoon baking soda

Directions:

1. Heat oven to 350F and line a baking sheet with baking paper.
2. In a bowl, cream peanut butter, and powdered Erythritol.
3. In a separate bowl, combine all dry ingredients.
4. Fold the dry ingredients into peanut butter and stir until you have a crumbly mix.
5. Stir in almond milk and roll dough into balls (2 tablespoons per cookie).
6. Drop dough onto baking sheet and flatten with a fork,

making a crisscross pattern.
7. Bake cookies 10 minutes. Cool completely before serving.

Nutrition analysis:

- High in vitamin E
- High in protein
- High in Omega-6

49. Comfort Cups

A neat looking meal is always appreciated, but sometimes we just have to get a bit messy. Anyway, who cares about neatness when you have a heavenly peanut butter-cacao dessert in front of you? No one, and neither will you once you try this simple yet delicious dessert.

Preparation time: 5 minutes + inactive time

Serves: 4

Ingredients:

- ¼ cup peanut butter
- 4 tablespoons coconut cream
- 4 tablespoons melted coconut oil
- 2 teaspoons cacao paste
- 8 drops Stevia

Directions:

1. Divide peanut butter between four silicone cups.
2. Divide remaining ingredients between the cups and stir to combine. Scrape down the cup sides.
3. Place in freezer 2 hours.
4. Remove from cups and serve.

Nutrition analysis:
- High in manganese
- High in vitamin E
- High in vitamin B6
- High in niacin

Sweet Fritters With Lime

Almond-flour based fritters with a refreshing lime icing. Simple, smooth, satisfying.

Preparation time: 5 minutes

Cooking time: 5 minutes

Serves: 9

Ingredients:
- ½ cup almond flour
- 3 tablespoons powdered Erythritol
- 1 teaspoon baking soda
- ½ teaspoon guar gum
- 1 tablespoons flax seeds + 3 tablespoons water
- ½ tablespoon finely grated lime peel
- ½ teaspoon vanilla paste
- 2 cup coconut oil, for frying

Icing:
- 3 tablespoons powdered Erythritol
- 1 tablespoon fresh lime juice

Directions:
1. In a small bowl, combine flax and water. Place aside for 15 minutes.
2. In a medium-sized bowl, whisk almond flour, Erythritol,

baking soda, guar gum, and lime peel.

3. Stir in flax mixture and vanilla paste.
4. Heat coconut oil in a small saucepan.
5. Drop batter by tablespoon into heated oil. Fry 2 minutes per side.
6. Repeat with remaining batter.
7. In the meantime, combine powdered Erythritol and lime juice until a smooth icing has formed.
8. Dip fritters into icing and arrange onto a plate.
9. Serve warm.

Nutrition analysis:

- High in omega-6
- High in vitamin E
- Moderate in omega 3

Made in the USA
Middletown, DE
09 June 2018